BREATH AND BREAD

Breath and Bread

Reflections on the Holy Spirit

Michele T. Gallagher

ALBA·HOUSE   NEW·YORK

SOCIETY OF ST. PAUL, 2187 VICTORY BLVD., STATEN ISLAND, NEW YORK 10314

ST PAULS

Library of Congress Cataloging-in-Publication Data

Gallagher, Michele, 1943-
    Breath and bread: reflections on the Holy Spirit /
  Michele T. Gallagher.
        p.   cm.
    Includes bibliographical references.
    ISBN 0-8189-0807-6
    1. Holy Spirit.   I. Title.
  BT121.2.G35   1998
    231'.3 — dc21   97-38962
                                                 CIP

Produced and designed in the United States of America by the
Fathers and Brothers of the Society of St. Paul,
2187 Victory Boulevard, Staten Island, New York 10314,
as part of their communications apostolate.

ISBN: 0-8189-0807-6

Printing Information:

Current Printing - first digit   1   2   3   4   5   6   7   8   9   10

Year of Current Printing - first year shown

1998   1999   2000   2001   2002   2003   2004   2005

For
my beloved husband
JAMES F. GALLAGHER
1927 - 1991

Shall I compare thee to a summer's day?
Thou art more lovely and more temperate.

(Shakespeare, *Sonnet 18*)

TABLE OF CONTENTS

Thou mastering me
God! Giver of breath and bread:
World's strand, sway of the sea;
Lord of living and dead;
Thou hast bound bones and veins in me,
fastened me flesh,
And after it almost unmade, what with dread,
Thy doing: and dost thou touch me afresh?
Over again I feel thy finger and find thee.

Gerard Manley Hopkins,
"The Wreck of the Deutschland"

PREFACE

O let everything that has breath,
let all living creatures praise
The Lord!
(Psalm 150)

I invite you, my readers, all you who have breath, to praise the Lord with me! Let us praise Jesus as Lord for it is he who breathed his holy and risen Spirit into us as his Easter gift to us. We cannot speak of the Holy Spirit without speaking of Jesus as Lord and sender of the Spirit. But Jesus is only Lord because he emptied himself taking the form of a slave and becoming of human estate. As one like us Jesus entered the jaws of death to trample death by his glorious resurrection.

And we cannot speak of the Holy Spirit except in the Spirit's relationship in love and community with the Father and the Son in the mystery of the Godhead — the mystery of Love. And we cannot speak of the mystery of the Love of the Godhead without including our own response to that Love, that is, our beseeching Father, Son, and Spirit to make their dwelling place with us. The Spirit too helps us in our weakness with groanings unutterable in speech and bids us to arise, hasten and come to be refreshed in his everlasting love. Let us hurry and run to him for life and love, for breath and bread.

I have attempted ever so feebly to present symbols, metaphors, and images of the Holy Spirit because as creatures seeing through a glass darkly we only have "hints and guesses" into the unfathomable mystery of the Holy Spirit. The "hints and guesses" I have chosen to express are the symbols, metaphors, and images of the Holy Spirit which may be seen as theological icons. These theological icons represent our relationship to the Holy Spirit. The Holy Spirit is "immortal diamond" and in the brilliance of the Spirit's own light I can only write about very few of the infinite refracted lights of this "immortal diamond" as I have known them in prayer.

In each Eucharist, in the breaking of the bread, Jesus breathes his holy and risen Spirit into us, making our dry bones live. In each Eucharist as we know the Lord Jesus and his holy and risen Spirit, they are for us the breath that is bread.

This attempt to express some moments of epiphany which the Holy Spirit prompted was born of many years of enjoying the splendid feast of Pentecost. I thank you for allowing me to share the fruit of my prayer with you and wish you the fullness of peace which the world cannot give: the abiding presence of the Easter Jesus and his holy risen Spirit. For this gift of the Spirit let all of us who have breath raise a joyful shout unto the Lord. Let us sing in jubilation!

> But what is "singing in jubilation?"
> It is to be unable to understand
>   and express in words
>   the song the heart sings.
>
> * * *
>
> Let us turn from syllables
>   and raise a cry of jubilation.
> The cry of jubilation is a sound
>   which means the heart is bringing forth
>   something ineffable.
> To whom is such a song better directed
>   than to the ineffable Spirit?
> If you cannot express him,
>   and yet may not be silent,
>   what is left but to cry in jubilation?
> What is left but for the heart to rejoice
>   in a song without words?
>
> (St. Augustine, *Commentary on Psalms*,
> On Psalm 32-33)

M.T.G.

Feast of Jesus Christ, King

BREATH AND BREAD

THE HOLY SPIRIT AS FIRE

Casting Fire Upon the Earth

> "I am come to light a fire on the earth.
>   How I wish the blaze were ignited!
> I have a baptism to receive.
>   What anguish I feel till it is over!
> Do you think I have come
>   to establish peace on the earth?
> I assure you the contrary is true;
>   I have come for division."   (Lk 12:49-51)

This saying of Jesus is not only enigmatic, it is also frightening and disturbing. Where is the gentleness of the Good Shepherd carrying the ewes in his arms? Where is the Jesus who embraced and blessed the children? — who touched the leper? — who opened the eyes of the blind man? — who wept at the death of his friend Lazarus? — who protected the woman taken in adultery? That kind and gentle Jesus is the same one who says, "I am come to light a fire on the earth."

But what does Jesus mean? John the Baptizer clearly tells us that Jesus will baptize with the Holy Spirit and with fire (cf. Mt 3:11; Mk 1:8; Lk 3:16; Jn 1:34). John's baptism was a baptism of repentance for he baptized only with water while preparing the way for Jesus to baptize with the Holy Spirit.

In order to unleash his spirit — the Holy

Spirit — on the world, the fire that would destroy evil and generate life and recreate the face of the earth, Jesus first had to undergo his own baptism that is, his death and resurrection. "Son though he was, he learned obedience from the things he suffered" (Heb 5:8). "He offered loud cries and tears to God… and he was heard because of his reverence" (Heb 5:7). The baptism of Jesus was his entering the jaws of death as every human being must do. No wonder Jesus cried out, "What anguish I feel till it is over!" The Son had emptied himself to take the form of a slave to enter death so as to vanquish that very enemy from which he, like every other human being, was wont to shrink. To give us the victory Jesus had to suffer death and all its griefs and pangs before he could be raised up by his Father.

When the Pharisees asked Jesus for a sign, he said no sign would be given them except the sign of Jonah. Jesus says,

> "This is an evil age.
> It seeks a sign.
> But no sign will be given
>   except the sign of Jonah." (Lk 11:29)

Matthew records it somewhat differently. Jesus says,

> "An evil and unfaithful age
>   is eager for a sign!
> No sign will be given it

except the sign of Jonah.
Just as Jonah spent
   three days and three nights
   in the belly of the whale,
so will the Son of Man
   spend three days and three nights
   in the bowels of the earth."   (Mt 12:39-40)

Here Jesus is referring to his mystical sleep in the grave from the time of his entombment to the morning of his resurrection. The mention of the three days between Jesus' death and resurrection is in the Synoptic tradition. It is well to note here that in the Johannine tradition Jesus' death, resurrection, glorification and sending of the Spirit take place all at once, in an instant, even though the first resurrection appearance is on "the first day of the week."

"The Son of Man had to suffer so as to enter into his glory" (Lk 24:26). He had to endure the anguish of suffering and death to become the risen and glorified Christ. He had to suffer to regain the glory he had with his Father before the world began (cf. Jn 17:5).

To cast fire upon the earth, the light of the Holy Spirit, Jesus' death and resurrection were necessary. John records that at the moment of Jesus' death,

He bowed his head
   and delivered over his spirit.   (Jn 19:30b)

John's recording the words "delivered over his spirit" are no accident. Jesus handed over to his Heavenly Father and at the same time to us his holy and risen Spirit from his open side. Thus the Holy Spirit was given to the world. The anguish of Jesus' baptism into death was over and in his moment of resurrection he released his Spirit. He did cast fire upon the earth! Now, as he had so wished, the fire was kindled — but only at the cost of his death. Sacrifice here is the price of Flame!

When Jesus says that he had come for division not for peace, he is saying that pain and passion must precede the Pentecost event. We are challenged and called to choose Jesus above all others to enter the reign of God. That is the meaning of Jesus' saying, "I have come for division." We may also say Jesus has come for separation — to separate us from the idols and the demons that beset us. When we have made the choice for Jesus, he will send his holy and risen Spirit to dwell in us bringing us peace.

But even as the icy grip of winter softens into the greening of spring and the fragrance of honeysuckle scents the air and robins return only to be glimpsed in their elusiveness, this peace for which we have renounced everything is as elusive as the robin on wing. This seems as if it were a contradiction. We do not make the decision for Jesus once. We are asked to live the time of our crisis and decision over and over again until we make the final act of choice and act of trust at the hour of our death.

This is not to say that we are always anguished nor is it to say we are always at peace. The peace of the Holy Spirit which the world cannot give is always with us but our eyes are held and we cannot always see that

> There lives the dearest freshness
> deep down things;
>
> * * *
>
> Because the Holy Ghost over
>   the bent
> World broods with warm breast
> And with ah! bright wings.
>
> ("God's Grandeur," Gerard Manley Hopkins)

Jesus allows us to glimpse moments of divine sweetness when he visits us in consolation, but these moments are brief and elusive and ineffable and over too soon. More often we know the anguish which Jesus felt — depression, grief, sadness, lone-liness, emptiness, abandonment, doubt, confusion, anxiety — in short the anguish of soul which even Jesus wanted to escape. Living this kind of poverty is the cost of discipleship and the cost of the anguish of being transformed into the glorified Christ.

Why, then, would one choose to become the glorified Christ if the price is so dear?

Love! The answer is love. And

> love consists in this:
> not that we have loved God,
>   but that he has loved us.   (1 Jn 4:10)

Or to state it another way, Jesus says,

"It was not you who chose me,
    it was I who chose you
        to go forth and bear fruit."   (Jn 15:16)

To all of us who are called to bear fruit Jesus has another message. He says,

"I am the true vine
    and my Father is the vine-dresser.
He prunes away every barren branch,
    but the fruitful ones
He trims clean
    to increase their yield."   (Jn 15:1-2)

To be "trimmed clean" is a painful process. The vine-dresser must cut us and wound us so that we will increase our yield. Jesus says,

"Your fruit must endure,
so that all you ask the Father
    in my name
        he will give you."   (Jn 15:16b)

We may ask the Father for "anything" and it will be given us. This however is to be read in context. We may ask for anything that will help us bear the fruit that will last. God our Father will never deny us the graces we need to fulfill his will for us — that is, our bearing fruit. The gift we need to ask for is the gift of the Paraclete, the Consoler, the

Comforter: the Holy Spirit. The Holy Spirit is the "*consolator optime,*" the ultimate consoler, while we patiently wait for the soil of our souls to produce its precious yield.

The Holy Spirit is given to each of us in every Eucharist for it is the Spirit of the risen and glorified Jesus which we receive when we eat his body and drink his blood. Abiding in Jesus as vine and branch we are so intimately one with him that his holy and risen Spirit is always being breathed into us (cf. Jn 20:22). Just as Jesus and the Father are one with the Holy Spirit, so in each Eucharist the Father, Son, and Holy Spirit come to us and make their dwelling place with us (cf. Jn 14:23).

When Jesus says he will cast fire on the earth, he is saying that he will send his Holy Spirit to us who may come as a searing flame scaring our psyche with the brand marks of Jesus. He may also come to us sweetly as the sun of justice with its healing rays. No matter how the Spirit comes — mightily or sweetly — we must always welcome him and allow him to cast his fire into our souls praying without ceasing,

Veni, Sancte Spiritus!
Come, O Holy Spirit!

THE HOLY SPIRIT AS REFRESHMENT

Thou Art More Lovely

Henry James once wrote that the two most beautiful words in the English language are "summer afternoon." When we hear these words, we conjure up images of leisure, linen, and fresh lemonade all under the protective shade of a leafy bower. A summer afternoon is a time for leisure and grace, pleasure and play, a time free from pressure and anxiety, a time to enjoy the glorious freedom of the children of God. Henry James most likely did not know he was describing a time of prayer graced by the gentle presence of the Holy Spirit. The summer afternoon of James' imagination and delight is the breath of the Holy Spirit.

But "what is so rare as a day in June" (James Russell Lowell)? We wait for it often too long. Lest we believe that our lives are an endless summer afternoon, Paul reminds us of our exile and our suffering and of the suffering of Jesus. Our lives are marked by toil as we wait for the ease of a summer afternoon. Paul expresses the same sentiment in this way:

> I consider the sufferings of the present
>   to be as nothing
> compared with the glory
>   to be revealed in us.   (Rm 8:18)

Paul reminds us that the Messiah had first to suffer so as to enter into his glory (cf. Lk 24:22) and that the path to sharing the glory of the risen Christ is the same for us and for all creation as well. Paul continues,

> Indeed, the whole created world
> eagerly awaits the revelation
>   of the children of God.
>
> Creation was made subject to futility,
>   not of its own accord
>   but by him who once subjected it;
> yet not without hope,
>   because the world itself will be freed
>   from its slavery to corruption
> and share in the glorious freedom
>   of the children of God.
>
> Yes, we know that all creation groans
>   and is in agony even until now.
> Not only that, but we ourselves,
>   although we have the Spirit as first fruits,
> groan inwardly while we await
>   the redemption of our bodies. (Rm 8:19-23)

This groaning of which Paul speaks and the agony we feel even until now is the pain of bearing fruit. This is the mystery of the grain of wheat which is the essence of the paschal mystery and the essence of gospel living.

Paul stresses that we are not delivered over to a futile way of life. Our groaning and agony are not in vain. We are called to hope and we have the ultimate gift, the Holy Spirit, to help us in our weakness. Paul continues,

> In hope we were saved.
>   But what is hope if its object is seen;
> How is it possible to hope for what one sees?
> And hoping for what we can not see
>   means awaiting it with patient endurance.
> The Spirit too helps us in our weakness,
>   for we do not know how to pray as we
> ought;
> But the Spirit makes intercession for us
>   with groanings unutterable in speech.
> He who searches hearts knows what the Spirit
>   means,
>   for the Spirit intercedes
>   for the saints as God himself wills.
>
>   (Rm 8:24-27)

Paul emphasizes that the Spirit helps us in our weakness. The all-knowing God who searches our hearts knows what we need and sends his Holy Spirit to pray in our hearts calling "Abba!" ("Father!"). To share in the glorious freedom of the children of God we need the Spirit to call out to the Father for us. Paul writes,

> All who are led by the Spirit of God
>   are children of God.
> You did not receive a spirit of slavery
>   leading you back into fear,
> but a spirit of adoption
>   through which we cry out, "Abba!"

(that is, "Father!").
The Spirit himself gives witness with our spirit
    that we are children of God.
But if we are children, we are heirs as well:
    heirs of God, heirs with Christ,
    if only we suffer with him
    so as to be glorified with him. (Rm 8:14-17)

The message is always the same. If only we suffer.... If only we suffer so as to be glorified with him. We do receive the glory but only if we suffer for a while. We bask in the glow of being a child of God with the Holy Spirit as proof. Paul writes,

The proof that you are children
    is the fact that God has sent forth his Son
    which cries out "Abba!" ("Father!").
You are no longer a slave but a child!
                     (Gal 4:6-7a)

The Spirit dwelling in us calling to the Father for us makes us children of God and heirs as well. The Spirit dwelling in us by virtue of the Eucharist gives us the light and warmth, comfort and grace, and rich ripe fruit of the lovely summer afternoon.

But what of the day when the leafy bower does not protect us and the heat scorches us, the linen is damp and uncomfortable and there seems as if there is no refreshment here below? We are parched and dry and empty. Has the Holy Spirit deserted us? Not at all! The Spirit needs to burn and sear our souls with a seraphic stigmata giving us the brand marks of Jesus to transform us into the likeness of the crucified and risen Lord. This is what it means to be an heir. We are heirs to the path of Jesus: his suffering, death, resurrection, and glorification. This is our legacy — the legacy of Jesus.

The Spirit needs to set himself as a seal on our hearts of wax. But if the heart be cold and the wax be hard, we need the fire of the Spirit to melt this wax so that, like a signet, his seal can be pressed into our hearts for all eternity. For only when the heart is set aglow, can the seal of the Holy Spirit be ever present. This flame is not always welcome, nor is it always comforting. It burns. It hurts just as the vine-dresser hurts us when he trims our fruitful branches clean so as to increase our yield of fruit (cf. Jn 15:1-2). The Holy Spirit expands our souls and fosters growth. And, as we know only too well, growth is painful. Jesus tells us,

> "I tell you truly:
>   you will weep and mourn
>   while the world rejoices;
> You will grieve for a time,
>   but your grief will be turned into joy.
> When a woman is in labor,
>   she is said that her time has come.
> When she has borne her child,
>   she no longer remembers her pain
>   for joy that a child has been born
>   into the world."   (Jn 16:20-21)

Yes, we will grieve, but Jesus assures us it is

only for a time. We will bear pain in order to yield fruit. This process is agonizing. But through all the pain the Holy Spirit has not abandoned us or left us orphaned (cf. Jn 14:18). He is always with us guiding the birthing of Christ in us. Although our eyes may be held and we cannot feel his presence, we must remember the promise of Jesus who says,

> "Behold! I am with you always
> until the end of the world." (Mt 28:20)

For the Holy Spirit is none other than the living power and force of the risen Jesus present on earth.

Even when we are parched and dry and the dew of the Holy Spirit seems all but lost to us, he is with us always as the "*consolator optime*," the best of comforters. The leisure, peace and grace of the lovely summer afternoon shall return to us. The Holy Spirit is that gentle breeze which refreshes and graces the summer afternoon, for of him Jesus says,

> "The wind blows where it will.
> You hear the sound it makes
>   but you do not know
>   where it comes from,
>   or where it goes.
> So it is with everyone
>   begotten of the Spirit." (Jn 3:8)

Although the Spirit can come as a driving wind tossing us into a hurricane of confusion, this is only for a while, for the Holy Spirit is the sweet zephyr of refreshment bringing us peace and joy, light and mildness. The Holy Spirit is more refreshing than the warm caress of a gentle breeze of a summer afternoon. As we know the sweet refreshment of the Holy Spirit in the breaking of the bread, we may say of the fair Spirit,

> Shall I compare thee to a summer's day?
> Thou are more lovely and more temperate.
>
> (Shakespeare, *Sonnet 18*)

THE HOLY SPIRIT AS UNGUENT

The Balm for Every Wound

On one occasion when a lawyer posed the question to Jesus, "Who then is my neighbor?" Jesus answered with the familiar parable of the Good Samaritan who was "moved with pity at the sight" of a man who fell prey to robbers. We are told specifically by Jesus that the Samaritan approached the battered man and "dressed his wounds, pouring in oil and wine" (cf. Lk 10:25-37). The wine containing alcohol was an antiseptic to prevent infection and oil was to soothe and comfort him. So it is with the oil of the Holy Spirit, that is, in liturgical usage, the oil of the sick and the oil of sacred chrism.

In biblical literature oil has always been an unguent to heal, a balm to soothe every wound. The Bride of Song of Songs says that the name of her beloved "is as oil poured out" (Sg 1:3). Oil not only soothes and heals the wounds of the flesh; it also brings joy and comfort to the spirit. Again, so it is with the Holy Spirit.

Now let us return to the use of oil for the sick. The ministers of the Church call upon the Holy Spirit to bless and sanctify this oil to soothe and comfort us. The Church prays,

God of all consolation,
You chose and sent your Son
   to heal the world.
Graciously listen to our prayer of faith:
Send the power of your Holy Spirit, the
      Consoler,
   into this precious oil,
   this soothing ointment,
   this rich gift,
   this fruit of the earth.

* * *

Make this oil a remedy
   for all who are anointed with it;
Heal them in body, in soul, and in spirit,
   and deliver them from every affliction.

(The Rites)

When a person who is sick in body or in mind is anointed with the blessed oil, the prayer is made beseeching the Holy Spirit,

Through this holy anointing
may the Lord in his love and mercy
help you with the grace of the Holy Spirit.

(The Rites)

The Holy Spirit in the liturgical life and practice of the Church is intimately associated with the symbol of oil.

The prayer after the anointing of the sick is most consoling.

Father in heaven,
   through this holy anointing

grant us comfort in our sufferings.
When we are afraid, give us courage,
    when afflicted, give us patience,
When dejected, afford us help,
    and when alone, assure us of the support
    of your holy people.   (*The Rites*)

When alone, we can also be assured of the divine presence of the Consoler. In these prayers for the sick the Church not only reflects but sacramentalizes the compassion and pity of Jesus who healed and

cured the people
    of every disease and illness.

* * *

They carried to him all those afflicted
    with various diseases and racked with pain;
    the possessed, the lunatics, the paralyzed.
He cured them all.   (Mt 4:23b-24)

Let us note that Matthew mentions the "lunatics." Who are these? Before the age of psychology and its lexicon, the "lunatics" are all those who suffer from emotional and psychological turmoil — the demons besetting every modern soul. When Jesus began to send out the Twelve "he gave them authority over unclean spirits," and told them to "anoint the sick with oil" (cf. Mk 6:7-13). By this oil of the sick — the balm for every wound — we are made whole to return to our mission of proclaiming the good news. This is to act in the image of Jesus.

Jesus refers to the Spirit and to his anointing with the oil of gladness when he inaugurated his ministry at Nazareth as recorded by Luke. Jesus says,

> "The spirit of the Lord is upon me,
>   therefore he has anointed me.
> He sent me to bring glad tidings to the poor,
>   to proclaim liberty to captives,
>   recovery of sight to the blind
>   and release to prisoners.
> To announce a year of favor from the Lord."
>   (Lk 4:18-19; cf. Is 61:1-3)

The prayer for the blessing of chrism speaks of oil as a source of "life and joy," a "gift of peace." The chrism gives those born of water and the Holy Spirit royal, priestly and prophetic character. It fills us with the power of the Holy Spirit and makes us temples of his glory.

The prophet and king, David, sang the praises of God specifically,

> You raise grass for the cattle,
>   and vegetation for our use,
> Producing bread from the earth,
>   and wine to gladden our hearts,
> So that our faces gleam with oil,
>   and bread fortifies our hearts. (Ps 104:14-15)

David sings of the bounty of the Lord and his manifold blessings — and not least among these are wine to cheer our hearts and oil to make our faces to shine. The wine, of course, is a reference to the Eucharist; the oil, to the assuaging gifts and presence of the Holy Spirit.

After the avenging flood the dove returned to Noah with an olive branch signaling that the wrath of God had ended and that peace and mercy had been restored to humankind. The olive branch, the source of the balm of forgiveness, is still a symbol of peace.

When Jesus was baptized in the Jordan by John, the voice of the Father was heard,

> "This is my beloved Son
>   in whom I am well pleased."
> And suddenly the sky opened and he [Jesus]
>   saw the Spirit of God
>   descend like a dove
>   and hover over him.
>
> (Mt 3:16-17; cf. Mk 1:9-11; Lk 3:21-22)

Or, as recorded in the Gospel of John,

> John the Baptizer gave this testimony also:
>   "I saw the Spirit
>   descend like a dove from the sky,
>   and it came to rest on him."   (Jn 1:32)

Here Jesus is anointed with the "oil of gladness" as Isaiah had foretold (cf. Is 61:1-3). The Spirit rushed upon Jesus and this was his anointing with the "oil of gladness."

We too are anointed with chrism, "the oil of

gladness," at our baptism. And as the rite for the blessing of chrism states

> when they [the faithful]
> are anointed with this holy oil,
> you make them temples of your glory.

Thus the oil of chrism or the "oil of gladness" makes us temples of the Holy Spirit. For Paul writes in his First Letter to the Corinthians,

> Are you not aware
>   that you are temples of God,
>   and that the Spirit of God dwells in you?
> If anyone destroys God's temple,
>   God will destroy him.
> For the temple of God is holy
>   and you are that temple.   (1 Cor 3:16-17)

And again the image of the temple is mentioned in the Letter to the Ephesians,

> Through him [Jesus],
>   the whole structure is fitted together
>   and takes shape
>   as a holy temple in the Lord;
> in him you are being built
>   into this temple
>   to become a dwelling place for God
>   in the Spirit.   (Eph 2:22)

The concept of anointing the temple is as old as the patriarchs — as old as Jacob, son of Isaac, son of Abraham. Let us recall Jacob's dream at Bethel.

The Holy Spirit as Unguent

When the sun had set, Jacob lay down and "taking
one of the stones of the shrine put it under his head."

> Then he had a dream:
> a stairway rested on the ground,
> with its top reaching to the heavens;
> and the angels of God
> were going up and down on it.
> And there was the Lord
> standing beside him and saying,

* * *

> "In you and your descendants
> all the nations of the earth
> shall find blessing.
> Know that I am with you;
> I will protect you wherever you go,
> and bring you back to this land.
> I will never leave you
> until I have done what I promise you."

> When Jacob awoke from his sleep,
> he exclaimed,
> "Indeed the Lord is in this place,
> and I knew it not."
> And trembling he said,
> "How awesome is this place!
> This is none other than
> the house of God
> and the gate of heaven!"
> Early the next morning Jacob took the stone
> that he had put under his head,
> set it up as a memorial stone,
> and poured oil on top of it.

(Gn 28:12-13a, 14b-18)

Notice that the Lord said to Jacob, "Know that I am with you." The Lord God was a "buckler and a shield" for Jacob (Ps 91:4) and the Lord God prom-ised to be with Jacob always in distress and in de-light. The abiding presence of the Almighty is com-forting and reassuring to Jacob. So comforting and consoling is the knowledge of the presence of the Almighty that Jacob cries out in "solemn won-der,"

> "How awesome is this place!
> This is none other than
> the house of God
> and the gate of heaven!"

Jacob in all his ecstasy erects a stone to mark the place and consecrates it a temple by the pouring of oil. This anointing marks this spot as a dwelling of the Almighty, a place where his presence abides. The liturgy still uses oil, which in the Church has always been traditionally associated with the Holy Spirit, to consecrate and dedicate a church. As the bishop pours chrism on the middle of the altar and its four corners and continues to anoint the whole table with oil, he prays,

> We now anoint this altar
>   and this building.
> May God in his power
>   make them holy and visible signs
>   of the mystery of Christ and the Church.
> (*The Rites*, II)

Jacob's anointing of the memorial stone pre-figures another anointing centuries later. At Bethany six days before Passover Jesus came to the house of Lazarus whom he had raised from the dead.

> There they gave him a banquet,
>   at which Martha served.
> Lazarus was one of those at table with him.
> Mary brought a pound of costly perfume
>   made from genuine aromatic nard
>   with which she anointed the feet of Jesus.
> Then she dried his feet with her hair,
>   and the house was filled
>   with the ointment's fragrance.   (Jn 12:2-3)

Mary was anointing the temple of Jesus' body. Did she recall Jesus' words at an earlier Passover? On that occasion Jesus said to the money changers,

> "Destroy this temple and
>   in three days,
>   I will raise it up."
> At this the Jews retorted,
>   "This temple
>   took forty-six years to build,
>   and you are going to raise it up
>   in three days!'"
> Actually Jesus was speaking about
>   the temple of his body.   (Jn 2:19-21)

Mary in her lavish profusion of love was extravagant in expressing her belief that Jesus was the Messiah, the Holy One of God. He was the new temple. And she knew — as Jacob had known in his dream — that she was in the presence of the Almighty. More than the ointment's fragrance filled the room and penetrated the hearts and souls of Mary and her sister Martha and their brother Lazarus. Mary knew in her heart when she saw Jesus,

> How awesome is this person!
> He is none other than the
>   Son of God!

After all, Jesus had told her earlier,

> "I AM
>   the resurrection
>   and the life."   (Jn 11:25)

And Mary knew he was the Messiah because she loved him almost as unconditionally as he had loved her.

We too are temples consecrated from the moment of our baptism when we were anointed with the oil of chrism. As was mentioned above, the Holy Spirit dwells in us. As his dwelling place we are consecrated temples as Paul reminds us,

> For the temple of God is holy,
>   and you are that temple.   (1 Cor 3:17)

As we are anointed with chrism, the "oil of gladness," in the royal, priestly, and prophetic office of Jesus, the Holy Spirit impels us to go forth to proclaim the good news — the good news that Jesus is risen and death shall be no more. After being buffeted and chaffed by the harsh winds of this world's coldness and bruised and cut by the sharp blows of cruelty we need to be assuaged by the oil and unction of the Holy Spirit to heal us and make us whole, if not in body, then surely in spirit. By virtue of the strength from the sacred balm for every wound, who is the Holy Spirit, we are convinced and are able to proclaim,

> "Death is swallowed up
>   in victory."

* * *

> Thanks be to God
>   who has given us the victory
>   through our Lord Jesus Christ.
>   (1 Cor 15:55, 57)

St. Ephraim, called the lyre of the Holy Spirit, tells us,

> That oil is a friend of the Holy Spirit.
> By means of the oil, the Holy Spirit
>   impresses His seal upon the sheep.
> Like a signet impressed in wax,
>   He impresses his seal.
> So also the invisible seal of the Spirit
>   is impressed on our bodies
>   with the oil with which we are anointed in
>   Baptism,
>   whereby we bear his seal.
>
>   (St. Ephraim the Deacon, from the
>   *Hymn on Oil and the Olive*, 4th century)

THE HOLY SPIRIT AS WATER AND LIGHT

The Fountain of Light

The eyewitness account of the martyrdom of Polycarp, second century bishop of Smyrna, is as follows.

As the amen soared up
    and the men at the fire set their light to it,
    a great sheet of flame blazed out.
And we who were privileged to witness it
    saw a wondrous sight.
The fire took the shape of a hollow chamber,
    like a ship's sail when the wind fills it,
    and formed a wall round about the martyr's
        figure;
and there he was in the center of it,
    not like a human being in flames
    but like a loaf being baked in the oven,
    or like a gold or silver ingot
    being refined in the furnace.
And we became aware of a delicious fragrance,
    like the odor of incense
    or other precious gums.
Finally when they realized
    that his body could not be destroyed by fire;
    the ruffians ordered one of the dagger-men
    to go up and stab him with a weapon.
As he did so, there flew out a dove,
    together with such a copious rush of blood
    that the flames were extinguished.

(*The Martyrdom of Bishop Polycarp*, 15, 16; 2nd century)

This account of the martyrdom of Polycarp is indeed charming. It may even be fanciful, but nonetheless it emphasizes the fecundity flowing from the open wound. Notice the imagery — "a dove flew out." This, of course, is reminiscent of the fecundity of the wound of the open side of Jesus. John records of Jesus,

> Then he bowed his head
> and delivered over his spirit.   (Jn 19:30)

The words "delivered over his spirit" are no accident, for in the Johannine Gospel the spirit is the Holy Spirit whom Jesus would give when he was glorified (cf. Jn 7:39). The death, resurrection, glorification, and the sending of the Spirit in the Johannine economy take place simultaneously — all at once, in an instant.

John continues,

> One of the soldiers
> thrust a lance into his [Jesus'] side
> and immediately blood and water
> flowed out.   (Jn 19:34)

Let us recall Jesus' words earlier that year at the Feast of Booths.

> On the last and greatest day of the festival,
> Jesus stood up and cried out.
> "If anyone thirsts, let him come to me;
> let him drink who believes in me.

Scripture has it:
    'From within him
    rivers of living waters shall flow.'"
(Here he was referring to the Spirit,
    whom those that came to believe in him
        were to receive.
There was, of course no Spirit as yet,
    since Jesus had not yet been glorified.)
                          (Jn 7:37-39)

Jesus invites us all to be refreshed by drinking from his open side, the fountain of salvation. Did Jesus recall at this time the words of the prophet Isaiah,

    "With joy you will draw water
      at the fountain of salvation"?   (Is 12:3)

Most likely he did, for the Holy One of Israel invites us to drink from his open side — to drink of the Holy Spirit — *fons vivus, ignis, caritas, et spiritalis unctio* — the fountain of life, fire, love, and spiritual unction or sweet anointing. We can not speak of the giving of the Spirit without speaking of the death, resurrection, and glorification of Jesus as Lord, and as sender of the Spirit.

From that stream flowing from Jesus' open side all creation is made new. For from before primeval dawn

    through him all things came
     into being,
    and apart from him

nothing came to be.
Whatever came to be in him,
    found life,
life for the light of all.   (Jn 1:3-4)

Here Jesus is the Word — the Logos — the Wisdom of God. Of him the sage of Proverbs writes,

The Lord begot me,
    the first born of his ways,
the forerunner of his prodigies
    of long ago;
From of old I was poured forth,
    at the first, before the earth.
When there were no fountains
    or springs of water;
    before the hills, I was brought forth;
While as yet the earth and the fields
    were not made,
    nor the first clods of the world.
When he established the heavens
    I was there,
when he marked out the vault
    over the face of the deep;
When he made the skies above,
when he fixed the foundations
    of the earth;
When he set for the sea its limits,
    so that the waters should not
    transgress his command;
Then I was beside him as his craftsman,
    and I was his delight day by day.
Playing before him all the while,
    playing on the surface of the earth."
        (Pr 8:22-31)

Jesus from all eternity was the craftsman of his Father for through him all things were made. He was and is and will always be the Creative Word. He was and is and always will be the delight of his Father — the pure joy who "does all things well" (Mk 7:37) and "makes all things new" (Rv 21:5). As the delight of the Father, Jesus "played" before the Father. To play is to enjoy — to be without anxiety — and to bask in that ease of relationship where there are no barriers because love is perfect. Herein is delight. This play and this delight exist quintessentially in the community of the Trinity, the Godhead. Every meaningful and significant human relationship holds this delight and this pleasure of play as an ideal for which to strive. Even in our individual relationships with God our prayer is play for we come before our God as his delight — for we know that his love for us is perfect. The Father delights in us beyond all our imagining!

From the torrent flowing from the side of Jesus all creation is reborn and is recreated in the Holy Spirit. That is what we mean when we pray,

Come, Holy Spirit, and renew the face of the earth.

Before the historical death and resurrection of Jesus all creation participated in this rebirth by anticipating the fruits of his resurrection, glorification, and sending of the Spirit. Because of the rush of the tide flowing from the side of Jesus — which is the fountain of life and light, that is, the person of the Holy Spirit — we can say figuratively that the grass is lush, the sky bright, the sea teams with life, the sun gives light, robins sing, dogwoods flower, the night sky is filled with stars. From the open side of Jesus every landscape in all variations is made new both on earth and beyond the earth. The Creative Word relights the suns and stars and moons in the constellations and galaxies still unknown to us. He refreshes the hills, for now by virtue of his resurrection and sending of the Spirit, they are clothed with rejoicing and all of us — all humankind — await the new form that he will give to this lowly body of ours made in the pattern of his own glorified body (cf. Ph 3:21). Thus we who are the Church, the bride of Christ, are reborn from his pierced side as Eve was brought forth from the side of Adam.

It is well here to return to the image of the dove mentioned in *The Martyrdom of Polycarp* and recall that the dove emerging from his wounded side symbolizes fecundity, and that fecundity is personified in the Holy Spirit, the fountain of life and light. This is what we mean when we cry out with joy in the Lord of Lords, the Lamb,

Behold! He makes all things new!   (Rv 21:5)

In the Lamb we rejoice praying,

How precious is your kindness, O God!
Your children take refuge

in the shadow of your wings.
They have their fill
    of the prime gifts of your house;
from your delightful stream
    you give them to drink.
For with you is the fountain of life,
    and in your light we see light.   (Ps 36:8-10)

For all the wondrous deeds of Jesus the Lamb and the Creative Word we praise him and hurry and run to him to drink from this fountain. St. Bonaventure expresses it in this way:

You soul devoted to God,
whoever you are,
run
with living desire
to this Fountain of life and light.

                    * * *

From the Fountain
flows the stream of the oil of gladness

                    * * *

the torrent, I say, of the pleasure of God,
from which the guests at the
heavenly banquet
drink to joyful inebriation
and sing without ceasing
hymns of jubilation.
Anoint us with this sacred oil
and refresh
with the longed-for waters of this torrent
the thirsting throat of our parched hearts,
so that amid shouts of joy and thanksgiving
we may sing to you

a canticle of praise,
proving by experience that
with you
is the fountain of life
and in your light
we shall see
light.

(St. Bonaventure, *The Tree of Life*, Sermon 47)

Bonaventure speaks eloquently and lyrically of Jesus and his Holy Spirit as the fountain of life and light. But what about the times we raise our cups to the open side of Christ in the Eucharist to drink deeply of his Spirit and we expect to be refreshed by this torrent of pleasure only to find that we drink a cup of suffering? We see no light and feel no consolation but only desolation. The darkness and dryness we experience is very real as is the listless spirit that makes us feel as if all that we are carrying in our bodies is the dying of Jesus (2 Cor 4:10). At these times, which seem to be more often than not, Jesus' yoke is not easy and his burden is not light. We feel oppressed and pray as Jesus did in his agony,

"Father, if it is possible,
    let this cup pass me by.
Still, let it be as you would have it,
    not as I." (Mt 26:42)

We search only to find more darkness. As Mary Magdalen sought Jesus at the tomb, she was weeping. She could not find him, but she perceived and finally did encounter him. Her unfulfilled desire grew. If it had failed when unfulfilled, it would not have been genuine desire. Anyone who seeks Jesus and finds him has been on fire with longing for him. Jesus asks Mary,

> "Woman, why do you weep?
> What are you looking for?" (Jn 20:13)

Jesus asks her in order that her desire may grow, for in naming him her love reaches a new intensity.

> Jesus said to her,
>   "Mary!"
> He had first called her simply
>   "Woman,"
>   and she did not recognize him;
> now he calls her by name,
>   as though to say,
>   "Recognize him who recognizes you.
> I know you,
>   not just as one woman among thousands,
>   but as yourself."
> Mary then immediately recognizes her Creator
>   and calls him,
>   "Rabboni,"
>   that is, "Teacher,"
> for he whom she sought was within her,
>   teaching her to seek.
> (Pope St. Gregory the Great, *Sermons on the Gospels*, No. 25)

When Jesus hides his face from us along with the consolation of his Holy Spirit, this only serves to

heighten the intensity of our love for him. We thirst
all the more as the psalmist says,

> As the deer longs for running waters,
> so my soul longs for thee, O God.   (Ps 42:2)

And again,

> O God, you are my God whom I seek;
>   for you my flesh pines
>   and my soul thirsts
>   like the earth
>   parched,
>   lifeless,
>   and without water.   (Ps 63:2)

Jesus and his holy and risen Spirit are the only
ones who can satisfy our thirst. Didn't Jesus promise
the Samaritan woman at the well,

> "Whoever drinks the water I give
>   will never be thirsty;
> no, the water I give
>   shall become a fountain within him,
> leaping up to provide
>   eternal life."   (Jn 4:14)

Jesus also thirsts for us to believe him. The
Preface for the Third Sunday of Lent says,

> In his thirst to receive her
>   [the woman of Samaria's] faith
> he awakened in her heart
>   the fire of divine love.

The genesis of this preface is St. Augustine's *Commentary on John.* Augustine writes,

> But Jesus who asked her for a drink
>   was really thirsting for her faith.
> Christ asks for water and promises water.
> He is in need and wants to receive;
> he is rich and wants to slake the thirst of others.
> "If thou didst know the gift of God," he says.
> God's gift is the Holy Spirit.   (*Treatise* 15)

This water of which Jesus speaks is the fountain of life. The Holy Spirit both refreshes us and causes us to thirst ever so much more for this living water, that is for Jesus and for himself. As Augustine says of himself and his own experience,

> You spread your fragrance,
>   and I drew breath
>   and kept sighing for you.
> I tasted,
>   and remain hungry and thirsty.
> You touched me,
>   and I have been set aflame in your peace.
>   (*Confessions*, St. Augustine, Book 7)

Although in each Eucharist we drink of the one Spirit, that is, the living water, we still thirst. We pray to the Spirit, "on our dryness pour thy dew" (*Veni, Sancte Spiritus*). Yes, in each Eucharist our thirst is quenched and, yes, in each Eucharist we thirst all the more until we drink of the "river of life-giving water, clear as crystal, which issues from the throne of God and the Lamb" (Rv 22:1). It is there that the risen Lord, the Lamb, tells us,

"Behold! I make all things new!
I am the Alpha and the Omega,
    the Beginning and the End.
To anyone who thirsts
    I will give to drink without cost
    from the spring of life-giving water."

(Rv 21:5-6)

The invitation is further extended.

The Spirit and the Bride say,
    "Come!"
Let the one who hears answer,
    "Come!"
Let the one who is thirsty come forward;
    let all who desire it
    accept the gift
    of life-giving water.   (Rv 22:17-18)

Only when we reach the New Jerusalem where "every tear shall be wiped away, and there shall be no more death or mourning, crying out or pain" (Rv 21:4), only then will we be satisfied drinking in joyful inebriation. And until that day we raise our cups to the open side of the risen Jesus to drink of his Spirit, for his Spirit is the fountain of life and light refreshing us on our pilgrim way. And until that day when we are called to drink from the river issuing from the throne of the Lamb, let us pray with the poet,

> O thou, Lord of life, send my roots rain.
>> (Gerard Manley Hopkins,
>> Sonnet, "Thou art indeed just")

THE HOLY SPIRIT AS KISS BETWEEN
THE FATHER AND THE SON

The Exquisite Embrace

"Let him kiss me with the kiss of his mouth."
(Sg 1:1)

So begins the beautiful, sensuous, and sensitive love poem, the Songs of Songs. In this poem the beloved expresses the desire of every human being — the desire to be loved. The natural expression of the love between two people is a kiss. "The touch of lips signifies the bringing together of souls" (Bernard of Clairvaux, *Sermon on Songs*, 2, III). This is the intimacy for which every person longs. The heart yearns to be known and to share the secrets of the soul with another — a beloved friend or spouse. Sometimes in the course of our lives we are blessed with the intimacy of such a rare relationship, perhaps only once or twice in a lifetime, but during our life's span these relationships are only for a while. The relationship may dissolve or be changed by death, and we suffer the loss of separation. This grief is indeed painful and quite difficult to bear. Qoheleth tells us,

There is a time to weep,
and a time to laugh,

a time to mourn,
    and a time to dance.
A time to scatter stones,
    and a time to gather them;
a time to embrace,
    and a time to be far from embraces.

(Ec 3:4-5)

More often than not, except for those who are exceptionally fortunate, our time is a time to be far from embraces — that is, the embrace of another human being. Fortunately, however, for all of us there is the divine embrace which is always extended to all of us. We are not always aware of it, nor do we always want it. We prefer a human embrace, but the embrace of God for us is always present to us, for our God loves us "with an everlasting love" (Jr 31:3). The intimacy we long for is "the love of God being poured forth in our hearts through the Holy Spirit who has been given to us" (Rm 5:5).

But how is this love given? How are we kissed by God? What is this kiss? Who is this kiss? The following thoughts are only my feeble attempts to plumb the mystery of the Trinity with the help of the theologies of St. Thomas Aquinas and St. Bernard of Clairvaux.

From all eternity the Father spoke and the utterance of his mouth was the eternal Word, the Son whom the Father had begotten and loved as himself. And from all eternity the Son loved the Father and the expression of that love was the Son's kissing the Father with the kiss of his mouth. That kiss is the person of the Holy Spirit. And from all eternity both the giver of the kiss and the kiss are ours. The Holy Spirit, the love between the Father and the Son, is the eternal and supreme kiss given to us when we pray,

> Let him kiss me with the kiss
> of his mouth.
>
> (cf. Bernard of Clairvaux,
> *Sermon on Songs*, 8)

The English language has only one word — "kiss" — to express every kind of embrace, but Latin employs two words, *suavis*, which means the tender, innocent, sweet kiss of a child, of a mother or father, of a beloved friend; and it employs the word *osculum* which means the passionate and ravishing kiss of a most beloved and cherished spouse. The supreme and eternal kiss which we receive, the object of our meditation in this chapter, is the Holy Spirit. This Holy Spirit is both *suavis* and *osculum*. The Holy Spirit is at one and the same time child and friend, mother and father, lover and spouse to us. We see this recorded in Scripture at the overshadowing of Mary by the Holy Spirit (cf. Lk 1:28-35). The Holy Spirit — the supreme kiss — ravished the soul of Mary and thus Jesus was conceived in her. So it is with us. When we are kissed by the supreme kiss, Jesus is conceived in us.

O admirable commercium!
O wonderful exchange!

This kiss assuages our loneliness, satisfies our longings, and consoles us as we wait in this exile for the ecstasy of the eternal and everlasting embrace when we shall see God face to face.

Each time we are kissed by the Holy Spirit, the supreme kiss, this same Holy Spirit speaks to us as the Bridegroom speaks to the Bride. As the lover of Songs speaks, the Holy Spirit says to us,

> "Arise, my beloved,
>   my beautiful one,
>   and come!
> For see,
>   the winter is past,
>   the rains are over and gone,
>   the flowers appear on the earth,
>   the time of pruning the vines has come,
>   and the song of the dove is heard in our
>   land.
> The fig tree puts forth its figs
>   and the vines, in bloom,
>   give forth fragrance.
> Arise, my beloved,
>   my beautiful one,
>   and come!
> O my dove in the clefts of the rock,
>   in the sweet recesses of the cliff,
> Let me see you,
>   let me hear your voice,

For your voice is sweet,
and you are lovely."

* * *

My lover belongs to me and I to him;
he browses among the lilies.

(Sg 2:10-14, 16)

Each of us is the Bridegroom's delight and thus the Holy Spirit's delight. The Holy Spirit delights in us for we are the work of his hands fashioned to be his Bride.[1] The Bridegroom continues,

"You are a garden enclosed,
a fountain sealed.

* * *

You are a garden fountain,
a well of living water,
streams flowing down from Lebanon.
Arise, O north wind, and come,
O south wind: blow through my garden
and let the aromatical spices thereof flow.
Let my lover come into his garden
and taste its rarest fruits." (Sg 4:12, 15-16b)

Here the pleasures of the garden, the symbol of the soul, are reserved for the Bridegroom and him

---

[1] The symbol of the Bride applies to men as well as to women because according to the imagery and language of the mystical tradition the soul is always feminine in relation to God.

alone. We are the delight of the Bridegroom — the Holy Spirit, as the Holy Spirit — the supreme kiss — is the ultimate delight for us.

The love of Father, Son, and Spirit for each of us is described by Jesus as he speaks of himself as the Good Shepherd. Jesus says,

> "I am the good shepherd
> I know my sheep
>   and my sheep know me
>   in the same way that the Father knows me
>   and I know the Father."   (Jn 10:14-15)

Here Jesus tells us he knows us. To "know" in the biblical sense is to know the beloved with even more intimacy than a bridegroom knows his bride. It is a knowledge of the heart. It is heart speaking to heart. It is deep calling to deep. It needs no words — has no words. It is ineffable! As Jesus says, he knows us as the Father knows him. Of this knowledge the Holy Spirit thus proceeded. "To know." then, is "to love." It is the love which probes the mind and searches the heart and whatever that love finds, to the lover it is ineffably beautiful. Jesus further tells us of this love. He says,

> "As the Father has loved me,
>   so I have loved you.
> Live on in my love."   (Jn 15:9)

Imagine! or is it beyond our imagining that Jesus loves us as the Father has loved him! That love as we discussed above is the force that begot the person of the Holy Spirit! This is the kiss of Jesus — it is his gift of the Holy Spirit whom he communicates to us in that supreme kiss when

> he breathed on them
>   [his disciples and us]
> and said:
>   "Receive the Holy Spirit."   (Jn 20:22)

Bernard of Clairvaux corroborates this as he writes,

> "He breathed on them," it says,
> and that certainly means on his apostles,
>   that is, the primitive Church, and said,
>   "Receive the Holy Spirit."
> That was the kiss.
> What was it?
>   A breath?
> No, but the invisible Spirit,
>   who is so bestowed in the breath of the Lord
>   that he is understood to have proceeded
>   from the Son as well as from the Father.
>   (cf. Jn 15:26) (*Sermon on Songs*, 8, I)

As Jesus is the revealer of the Father so also is he the revealer of the Spirit. Luke records that Jesus "rejoiced in the Holy Spirit" and said,

"I offer you praise, O Father,
    Lord of heaven and of earth,
because what you have hidden
    from the learned and the clever
    you have revealed to the merest children.
Yes, Father you have graciously willed it so.
Everything has been given over to me by my
        Father.
No one knows the Son except the Father
    and no one knows the Father except the Son
    and anyone to whom the Son wishes to reveal
        him."
Turning to his disciples he said to them
privately:
    "Blest are the eyes that see what you see.
    I tell you many prophets and kings wished
        to see what you see but did not see it,
        and to hear what you hear but did not
            hear it."   (Lk 10:21-24)

Again, Jesus uses the word "know" in the most
intimate sense to tell us of the privilege of his
disciples and of our privilege. Jesus says that we
know him and we know the Father. To know the
Father and the Son is also to know the Holy Spirit.
What many a prophet and many a king has longed
to see and to hear, we do see and hear and feel. What
we see and hear and feel is the supreme kiss — it is
the Holy Spirit.

Again, let us return to Bernard's sermon.

    … and he [Jesus] made him [the Spirit] known
        to John the Evangelist,

the disciple Jesus loved (Jn 13:23).
For his soul [John's]
    was pleasing to the Lord (Ws 4:14),
        and worthy
    both of the dowry and the name of a Bride;
        deserving the Bridegroom's embraces
        and worthy to recline
            on the Bridegroom's breast (Jn 13:25).
John learned
    from the heart of the only-begotten
        what he had learned from his Father.
Not he alone, but all those
    to whom the Angel of Great Counsel (Is 9:6)
    said,
        "I call you friends,
            for all that I have heard from my Father
            I told you" (Jn 15:15).

(Sermon on Songs, 8, VI)

All of us wish to be John and have his intimacy with the Lord wherein the Lord will reveal to us the secrets of the kingdom as he did to John. Again in Bernard's sermon we encounter the word "know." Jesus has made his Spirit known to John. He therefore gave him the kiss! At each Eucharist we too receive the kiss as the Lord fills us with his holy and risen Spirit. We pray as we approach him,

You, I carry, O Lord,
    in the cup of my hand,
I adore you, my God,
    who rest upon my lips.
You whom the world

could not hold in its limits,
You whom heavens and earth proclaim,
    joyously singing,
You, my Lord,
    I receive in my heart!

> (Lucien Deiss, adapted from
> Communion Prayer of the Marionite Liturgy)

At each Eucharist we know that we open our mouths and the Risen Lord fills them (cf. Ps 82:11). He opens his hand and satisfies the desire of every living thing (cf. Ps 104:28). With all passion and ardor at each Eucharist let us thank and adore Father, Son, and Spirit saying,

"Kiss me with the kiss of your mouth."

And we know that the kiss of the Lord's mouth is the exquisite embrace of the crucified. Thus we assume the posture of the cruciform — our wounds commingling with his. This is the kiss, and in this kiss the Eucharistic Jesus is

honey in the mouth
music to the ear
a shout of gladness in the heart.

> (St. Bernard of Clairvaux,
> *Sermons on the Holy Name of Jesus*)

THE HOLY SPIRIT AS
FINGER OF GOD'S RIGHT HAND

"And Dost Thou Touch Me Afresh?"

> Thou mastering me
> God! giver of breath and bread;
> World's strand, sway of the sea;
> Lord of living and dead;
> Thou hast bound bones and veins in me,
> fastened me flesh,
> And after it almost unmade, what with dread,
> Thy doing: and dost thou touch me afresh?
> Over again I feel thy finger and find thee.
>
> (Gerard Manley Hopkins,
> "The Wreck of the Deutschland," Stanza I)

The God of whom Gerard Manley Hopkins writes is the God whom we adore as all-powerful and all-gentle. This is the God of mystery — profound mystery before whom we bow low, and yet for all his mastery over us, we feel his finger. The image of the finger is an allusion to the *digitus Paternae dexterae*, "the finger of God's right hand." In the corpus of liturgical literature on the Holy Spirit, "the finger of God's right hand" is the Holy Spirit as sung in the ancient chant, *Veni, Creator Spiritus* (Come, Creator Spirit). The poet writes,

> Over again I feel thy finger and find thee.

To feel the finger or the touch of the Holy Spirit is to find or to know God in all his profundity. The finger of God's right hand may touch us "afresh" with a most gentle touch or may touch us with searing flame. No matter. However the Holy Spirit touches us, we must submit to his promptings because he is the "mastering" God. But isn't this too much to ask? Why submit to a mastering God — a God who can inflict pain and at the same time bind up our wounds? Or as Hosea writes,

> Come, let us return to the Lord,
>   for it is he who has rent,
> but he will heal us;
> he has struck us,
>   but he will bind our wounds.   (Ho 6:1)

Why have a God that is called "Thou mastering God" at all? This "mastering" God demands total surrender to his will. We are wont to shrink from this all-powerful God unless we understand that this "mastering" God is the God who is the "world's strand and sway of the sea." It is he who flung the constellations into their places in the heavens, who set for the sea its limits, who chartered the planets in their course, who set the circuit of the stars, who lit the luminaries of the firmament, or to say it as Dante did,

> It is Love who lights the sun
> and the other stars.   (*Paradiso*, xxxiii)

And this God who is so wondrous is Love. If he can "tell the number of the stars and call each by name" (Ps 147:4), he can guide the paths of our lives weaving them into a tapestry befitting the palace of a king — no, not merely a king, but the King of Kings. We can trust the number and sum of our years to a God who is so immense that "a thousand years in his sight are as yesterday, now that it is past, or as a watch of the night" (Ps 90:4). This great and awesome God is to be adored. We need to plunge into contemplation of the divine goodness, that bottomless and shoreless sea, to know that his love for each of us is as awesome as his power. This great, terrible, awesome, and powerful God is the same God who breathed life into the nostrils of the first human being, Adam, (cf. Gn 2:7) and formed each of us in our mothers' wombs. He "hast bound bones and veins in me," and "fastened me flesh." The psalmist expresses the same sentiment thus:

> O Lord, you have probed me
>   and you know me;
> you know when I sit and when I stand;
> you understand my thoughts from afar.
> My journeys and my rest you scrutinize,
>   with all my ways you are familiar.
> Even before a word is on my tongue,
> behold, O Lord, you know the whole of it.
>
> * * *
>
> Truly you have formed my inmost being;
>   you knit me in my mother's womb,

I give you thanks that I am fearfully,
   wonderfully made;
   wonderful are your works.
My soul also you knew full well;
   nor was my frame unknown to you
When I was made in secret,
when I was fashioned in the depths of the
earth.

                        (Ps 139:1-4, 13-15)

This God — this "mastering" us God — is to be adored. We must first bow low in profound adoration and wonder and then and only then can we trust his ways to order our lives. God's providence over us is also mystery demanding wonder, adoration, and trust.

The God who breathed into the nostrils of Adam making him a living being is the same God, the risen and glorified Jesus, who breathes ever so intimately into us saying,

   "Receive the Holy Spirit."   (Jn 20:22)

As we are filled with the light and life of the Holy Spirit and his finger "dost touch" us "afresh," we are "clothed with power from on high" (Lk 24:49) to trust our whole lives to him and offer our first fruits to him. To offer first fruits is to offer the pleasing sacrifice of Abel. Abel generously offered not just one lamb to God, but in offering his first fruits, in symbol, he offered everything — his whole flock of sheep and eventually himself to the Lord

God (cf. Gn 4:6). How can we be so generous? How can we trust so completely? We can only do this when we know that the God of creation is the God of redemption. And redemption is love. "Jesus did not deem equality with God something to be grasped at, but emptied himself taking the form of a slave." He was known to be of "human estate" and it was "thus that he humbled himself, obediently accepting even death, death on a cross!" (Ph 2:6-8). Jesus gave up the glory he had with his Father before the world began (cf. Jn 17:5) in order to trample death by his death that we might have eternal life, so much did he love us. So much did the Son love us that he promised us another Advocate, another Paraclete, another Consoler, another Comforter — his holy and risen Spirit. And that holy and risen Spirit, the finger of God's right hand, is Love.

Only in the climate of profound adoration and wonder at the infinite immensity of God's love for each of us personally can we be prompted to make an act of profound trust and total surrender to our "mastering" God. This act of total surrender and trust is usually made in vow — be it vow of religious profession, vow of marriage — or more fundamentally vow of baptism. And the vow is not made once but renewed over and over again until we make the final act of trust at the moment of death. Very often we consecrate our lives to God in vow or commitment in youthful enthusiasm and do not realize that the daily living of that commitment demands discipline and can often become tedious. Yet when we renew our offering, we renew our idealism and restore the joy of our youth. The once bright embers of our first fervor are fanned into flame. We pray in the Roman Canon for the Lord God to accept our offerings as he once accepted the gifts of his servant Abel. When we offer our first fruits, we are Abel, the eternal youth. We are, then, forever young.

Let us return to examine our baptismal vow or commitment. *Bapto* the Greek verb, literally means "to be dipped into." When we are baptized into Christ, we are dipped into his death and resurrection. Paul tells us in the Letter to the Romans,

> Are you not aware that we
>   who are baptized into Christ Jesus
>   were baptized into his death?
> Through baptism into his death
>   we were buried with him, so that,
>   just as Christ was raised from the dead
>   by the glory of the Father,
>   we too might have a new life.
> If we have been united with him
>   through likeness to his death,
>   so shall we be through a like resurrection.
>   (Rm 6:3-5)

We first receive the Holy Spirit in the sacrament of baptism. As the celebrant blesses the water, he prays,

The Holy Spirit as Finger

We ask you, Father, with your Son,
   to send the Holy Spirit
   upon the water of this font.
May all who are buried with Christ
   in the death of baptism
   rise also with him to newness of life.

(*The Rites*)

After having been baptized in the name of the Father, Son, and Holy Spirit, the celebrant anoints the newly baptized with oil of chrism, "the oil of gladness," with these words,

God the Father of our Lord Jesus Christ
   has freed you from sin,
   given you a new birth
      by water and the Holy Spirit,
   and welcomed you into his holy people.
He now anoints you
   with the chrism of salvation.
As Christ was anointed
   Priest, Prophet, and King,
so may you live always
   as members of his body,
   sharing ever-lasting life. (*The Rites*)

The commitment made at baptism needs to be renewed over and over again. If we are to receive the Holy Spirit and be anointed as prophet, priest, and royal children of the Father, we assume the role that Jesus assumed at his own baptism. At his baptism by John in the Jordan, Jesus heard the voice of the Father and saw the Spirit descend from the heavens.

> After Jesus was baptized,
>   he came directly out of the water.
> Suddenly the sky opened
>   and he saw the Spirit of God
>   descend like a dove and hover over him.
> With that, a voice from the heavens said,
>   "This is my beloved Son.
>   My favor rests on him."   (Mt 3:16-17)

As the moment of his baptism Jesus was favored and this meant he acquired the certainty that he was to assume the role of the Servant of Yahweh as foretold by Isaiah,

> Here is my servant whom I uphold,
>   my chosen one with whom I am pleased,
>   upon whom I have put my Spirit,
> he shall bring forth justice to the nations,
>   not crying out, not shouting,
>   not making his voice heard in the street.
> A bruised reed he shall not break,
>   and a smoldering wick he shall not quench,
> Until he establishes justice on the earth;

* * *

> I, the Lord, have called you [the Servant]
>   for the victory of justice,
> I have grasped you by the hand;
> I formed you, and set you
>   as a covenant for the people,
>   a light for the nations,
> To open the eyes of the blind,

to bring out prisoners from confinement,
and from the dungeon,
        those who live in darkness.

(Is 42:1-4a, 6-7)

We know that Jesus could not bring light and life to us unless he first entered darkness and death only to conquer it by his own suffering, death, and resurrection. This is what Isaiah called "the victory of justice."

At his baptism Jesus made the act of total surrender to be the servant of his Father, and so in our baptism we are anointed to be servants of the Father. We need to make the act of total surrender. This is indeed difficult and the Father knows that we need a sign to know our offering is accepted and acceptable to him. Jesus did too.

"About eight days after saying" that he, the Son of Man, "must first endure many sufferings, be rejected by the elders, the high priests and the scribes, and be put to death, and then be raised up on the third day" (Lk 9:21), Jesus took Peter, James and John and went up on to a mountain to pray, no doubt led by the Spirit.[1]

There while he was praying,
        his face changed in appearance
        and his clothes became dazzlingly white.

* * *

---

[1] Jesus was led by the Spirit into the desert to pray (Lk 4:1) and he "rejoiced in the Spirit" to praise his Father (cf. Lk 10:21).

Then from the cloud came a voice
    which said,
        "This is my Son, my Chosen One.
            Listen to him."   (Lk 9:29, 35)

Here Jesus was transfigured by the Holy Spirit. He was given a taste of his resurrection in a glorified body to strengthen him for the scandal of the cross. Jesus was given divine consolation, the touch of the Holy Spirit, before he offered his vow to the Father — the most perfect vow — his life for our ransom.

The voice from the cloud and the implied presence of the Holy Spirit, the light which transfigured his body, is similar and reminiscent of his baptism. Here Jesus, the Suffering Servant, prepares to say to his Father,

"Father, into your hands
    I commend my spirit."
                    (Lk 23:46; cf. Ps 31:6)

Before we offer our vow or before we are asked to endure some trial to live our commitment to the full, we are often given a glimpse of gladness. We are given divine consolation in prayer. We can almost taste the sweetness of the Lord. The finger of the Holy Spirit touches us "afresh" and ever so sweetly and delicately. This is to strengthen us and to reassure us that amid all trials and sufferings — no matter how heavy the cross — "all shall be well" (Juliana of Norwich). Why? Because the risen Lord and his Holy Spirit are with us. God assures us in unspeakable intimacy,

> "I know you."
> "I am with you."
> "I AM."

This is a quiet and joyful ecstasy — a silence full of bells! This experience of divine sweetness in the Lord is ineffable — it can only be *known* with a knowledge of the heart. It is known in the depths of our being and there are no words to describe it — just as Moses could find no words, but only stand in wonder at the sight of the burning bush.

> There the Lord appeared to him
> in a flame of fire out of the midst of a bush.
> As he looked on he was surprised
> to see that the bush, though on fire,
> was not consumed.
> So Moses decided,
> "I must go over to look at this remarkable sight,
> and see why the bush is not burned."
> (Ex 3:2-3)

God lets us wonder at his presence. We are awed by the finger that touches us "afresh," just as Moses. We contemplate the defiance of nature to see a bush set aflame and yet its leaves not wither. Amid the flames the leaves are moist with the dew of the Holy Spirit.

Amid this wonder we strive to make our offering or vow a total holocaust. We pray,

> "To do your will, O God,
>   is my delight." (Ps 40:9)

We wish to have the attitude of Jesus who said,

> "The One who sent me is with me.
> He has not deserted me
>   since I do always the things that please
> him." (Jn 8:29)

Jesus obeys the Father. Let us return to Psalm 40. The psalmist prays,

> Sacrifice or oblation you wished not,
>   but ears open to obedience you gave me.
> Holocausts or sin offerings you sought not;
> Then said I,
>   "Behold I come;
>   in the written scroll it is prescribed for me,
> To do your will, O God, is my delight,
>   and your law is within my heart."
>   (Ps 40:7-9)

We have just mentioned that we offer our lives as a holocaust and yet the psalmist writes, "holocausts or sin offerings you [God] sought not." These are the sacrifices of the old law, "the blood of bulls and goats" (Heb 10:4), which have been replaced by "the offering of the body of Jesus Christ once for all" (Heb 10:10).

Jesus' offering was a sacrifice of praise and an act of perfect obedience, but it was not without anguish. Earlier the homilist of Hebrews tells us,

> In the days when he [Jesus] was in the flesh,
>   he offered prayers and supplications
>   with loud cries and tears to God,
>   who was able to save him from death;
> And he was heard because of his reverence.
> Son though he was, he learned obedience
>   from what he suffered;
> And when perfected,
>   he became the source of eternal salvation
>   for all who obey him.   (Heb 5:7-9)

We must remember the words of the poet,

> Thou has bound bones and veins in me,
>   fastened me flesh,
> And after it almost unmade, what with dread,
> Thy doing.

Yes, the God who fashioned in secret does crush us to infirmity (cf. Is 53:10a) as he was "pleased" to crush his Suffering Servant, Jesus, to infirmity so that "the will of the Lord may be accomplished through him" (Is 53:10b). The Lord who made us will almost unmake us to accomplish his will in us — to make us a sacrifice of praise. And note that the poet adds "what with dread." The suffering we will be asked to endure is indeed dreaded. Jesus dreaded his agony. He tells us,

"I am come to cast fire on the earth,
    and how I wish the blaze were ignited!
I have a baptism to receive
    and what anguish I feel till it is over!"
                                    (Lk 12:49-50)

To fulfill our baptismal vow we too will feel anguish, but we too will become a sacrifice of praise.

It is interesting to note here that the ultimate root of the English word "vow" is taken from the Sanskrit verb, *ohate*, literally meaning, "he praises." Let us remember the words of the psalmist,

The one who offers praise as a sacrifice
    glorifies me.   (Ps 50:23)

The sacrifice of praise offered by the Blessed Virgin Mary was a perfect act of obedience, and although her "yes" caused great joy for through it and by it she conceived the Christ, it also caused great pain. Simeon told her, "your own soul a sword shall pierce" (Lk 2:23), for

when the soul says "yes" to God,
    unconditionally,
He always takes her at her word.[2]

Mary's offering of praise, her act of obedience,

---

[2] Mother M. Justin McKiernan, O.S.U., *Venerable Marie of the Incarnation* (New Rochelle, NY: College of New Rochelle, 1949), p. 13.

was also a martyrdom in spirit because she surrendered herself totally to God with such love and affection (cf. Bernard of Clairvaux, *Sermons within the Octave of the Assumption,* 14-15). Mary felt the finger of the Holy Spirit as he touched her "afresh" with delight and "what with dread." So it is with us. In each Eucharist we are touched by the Holy Spirit filling us with life and light, as "giver of breath and bread."

Yes, we will always be touched "afresh" and will find God, but not always as the God of consolation. There will be moments of dread as the finger of God's right hand — the Holy Spirit — almost "unmakes" us. He asks us to be crushed over again, to be ground as pure bread for Christ (Ignatius of Antioch, *Letter to the Romans,* Chap. 6). This is the mystery of the grain of wheat that must fall into the ground and die in order to bear very much fruit (cf. Jn 12:24). We must remember and be reassured as Paul encouraged the Corinthians,

> We are afflicted in every way possible,
> > but we are not crushed;
> full of doubts,
> > we never despair.
> We are persecuted,
> > but never abandoned;
> we are struck down,
> > but never destroyed.
> Continually we carry about in our bodies
> > the dying of Jesus,
> so that in our bodies,

the life of Jesus may also be revealed.
(2 Cor 4:8-10)

Whether in consolation or desolation our God is with us. We are touched "afresh" with dread or with delight. The same finger who sears our souls and psyches also makes us whole. The gentle finger fashions us as clay in the hands of the potter (cf. Jr 18:1-6) making us beautiful as a bride adorned for her husband. (cf. Rv 21:2). These are the same gentle fingers of Jesus who "put those fingers" into the deaf-mute's ears and mouth, and "spitting touched his tongue; then looked up to heaven and emitted a groan, saying to him, 'Ephphata!' that is, 'Be thou opened!'" (cf. Mk 7:31-37). These same fingers open our ears to hear God's word and loose our tongues to proclaim his praise. And again we see the image of the gentle finger in the familiar parable of the rich man and Lazarus (cf. Lk 16:19-31). In our dread and desolation and dryness we call out to the Holy Spirit as did the rich man, Dives, to Abraham in whose bosom the poor man, Lazarus, was resting. We call out as Dives,

> "Father Abraham,
>   have pity on me.
> Send Lazarus
>   to dip the tip of his finger in water
>   to refresh my tongue,
>   for I am tortured in these flames."
> (Lk 16:24)

Although the "tip of the finger" of which Dives speaks is the finger of Lazarus, Lazarus here in his mercy is the symbol of the Holy Spirit, the Consoler. We ask this Holy Spirit in our tortured and anguished desert moments of aridity of soul when we long for water as the deer yearns for running streams to touch us with his gracious and gentle finger. We ask the Holy Spirit to refresh us with even a single drop of the dewy freshness of his grace, the waters of consolation, to moisten our parched tongues and to quench our thirsting spirits. We pray to the Holy Spirit to touch us "afresh" as we say,

> on our dryness pour thy dew.
> *(Veni, Sancte Spiritus!* Come, Holy Spirit!)*

The poet also calls the "mastering" God, "Lord of living and dead." Let us remember,

> None of us lives as his own master,
>   and none of us dies as his own master.
> While we live,
>   we are responsible to the Lord,
> And when we die,
>   we die as his servants.
> Both in life and in death
>   we are the Lord's.
> That is why Christ came to life again,
>   that he might be Lord
>   of both the dead and the living.
>   (Rm 14:7-9)

Both in life and in death we bow low in profound adoration to the "mastering" us God. To him through the prompting of the finger of his right hand, we offer a sacrifice of praise — our vow. We cannot question what the Lord gives and the Lord takes away. (cf. Job 1:21). The finger of God's right hand is present in the gentle zephyr of spring as well as in the raging tempest and winter storm. Hence, we accept whatever the Lord sends — dread or delight — either willingly or reluctantly. This is our vow. In all things we praise him. Let us pray the prayer of Peter,

> "Lord, to whom shall we go?
> You alone have the words
> of eternal life."   (Jn 6:68)

And again it was Peter who said to the Risen Lord when Jesus asked him, "Do you love me?"

> "Lord, you know all things.
> You know well that I love you."   (Jn 21:7)

Let us trust in the "mastering" God "who knows all things" and pray to his Holy Spirit,

> and dost thou touch me afresh?
> Over again I feel thy finger and find thee.

Yes, feeling the finger with either dread or delight we know that one day we will be sure to find that Spirit resting not as Lazarus in Abraham's bosom, but comforted in the soft pinions of the Holy Spirit's "warm breast and ah! bright wings" (Gerard Manley Hopkins, "God's Grandeur").

THE HOLY SPIRIT AS DELIGHT

Mentis Jubilatio!
(The heart's delight and the soul's jubilee!)

Philip sought out Nathanael and told him,
"We have found the one Moses spoke of in the
law,
    the prophets, too —
    Jesus, son of Joseph, from Nazareth."
Nathanael's response to that was,
    "Can anything good come from Nazareth?"
and Philip replied,
    "Come, see for yourself."
When Jesus saw Nathanael coming toward him
    he remarked:
"This man is a true Israelite.
    There is no guile in him."
"How do you know me?" Nathanael asked
him.
"Before Philip called you," Jesus answered,
    "I saw you under the fig tree."
"Rabbi," said Nathanael,
    "You are the Son of God;
        you are the king of Israel."
Jesus responded:
    "Do you believe
        just because I told you I saw you
        under the fig tree?
    You will see much greater things than that."
He went on to tell them,
    "I solemnly assure you,
        you shall see the sky opened,

and the angels of God
   ascending and descending
   on the Son of Man."   (Jn 1:45-51)

This call of Nathanael is indeed mysterious. What does Jesus mean when he says to Nathanael,

"Before Philip called you,
I saw you under the fig tree"?

Let us examine the Greek text to unlock this enigmatic response of Jesus to Nathanael. The verb "saw" is translated from the Greek verb *eidon* whose root is the verb *horao*. *Horao* not only means to "see" as to notice with the senses, but it carries the more profound meaning of "perceive," "understand," "recognize," and "know." So, let us rewrite the sentence,

"Before Philip called you,
I *knew* you under the fig tree."

To know here means to have intimate knowledge and as predicated of Jesus to know means to have divine omniscience. Jesus "knew" Nathanael from all eternity. Of Jesus, the Creative Word, it is written in Proverbs,

"The Lord begot me, the first born of his ways,
   the forerunner of his prodigies of long ago;
From of old I was poured forth,
   at the first before the earth.

* * *

When he established the heavens I was there;
When he marked out the vault over the face of
the deep,
When he made firm the skies above,
When he fixed fast the foundations of the
earth,
When he set for the sea its limits
   so that the waters should not transgress his
   command;
Then was I beside him as his craftsman,
   and I was his delight day by day,
Playing before him all the while,
   playing on the surface of the earth."

(Pr 8:22-23, 27-31)

The description of the Creative Word from Proverbs says that not only was Jesus the Son of God, the craftsman of the universe, but it implies that as the divine Son of God he "knew" each human being, each one of his disciples, each one of us from all eternity. As Jesus was begotten from "long ago," that is, from all eternity, he also "knew" not only the universe but each person who would dwell therein.

After Jesus tells Nathanael that he "knew him under the fig tree," Nathanael is awakened by the call of Jesus to recognize or to *know* Jesus as the Son of God. Nathanael says,

"Rabbi, you are the Son of God."   (Jn 1:49)

What awe Nathanael must have felt in stand-

ing in the presence of the divine! Didn't he wonder
at Jesus' words? Didn't he wonder at how Jesus
knew him? Wasn't he flattered and overjoyed that
the Son of God "knew" him, Nathanael, not for
anything he had done but simply because Jesus
chose him and loved him for who he was? Nathanael's
awe and wonder is expressed in his almost under-
stated confession of faith,

> "Rabbi, you are the Son of God."   (Jn 1:49)

This confession of faith is similar to Peter's.
After Jesus had offered his flesh as real food and his
blood as real drink, some of his disciples "broke
away from him" because of his "hard sayings." Jesus
then said to the Twelve,

> "Will you also go away?"
> Simon Peter answered,
> "Lord, to whom shall we go?
> You have the words of eternal life.
> We have come to believe;
>   we are convinced
>   you are God's holy one."   (Jn 6:68-69)

Nathanael's wonder and delight are also similar to that of the Samaritan woman at the well. After
Jesus offered her living water and told her about her
past, she said to him,

> "I know a Messiah is coming.
>   When he comes, he will tell us everything."

Jesus replied,
  "I who speak to you am he."   (Jn 4:25-26)

In her wonder and surprise and joy the Samaritan woman left her water jar and went out into the town to share her good news. She said to the people,

  "Come and see someone
    who told me everything I ever did!
    Could this not be the Messiah?"   (Jn 4:29)

Jesus knew her and she felt overjoyed to know and be known by him.

The man born blind had a similar reaction to Jesus. Of course, it was only natural to rejoice that his sight had been restored, but he was also expelled from the synagogue.

  When Jesus heard of his expulsion,
    he sought him out and asked him,
      "Do you believe in the Son of Man?"
  He answered,
    "Who is he, sir, that I may believe in him?"
  Jesus replied,
    "He is speaking to you now."
  He said, "I do believe, Lord."
    He bowed down to worship him.
                                  (Jn 9:35-38)

Now the man born blind could see not only with his senses, but he could see and know the Messiah — Jesus — as the divine Son of God!

Martha and Mary, who were intimate friends of Jesus, did not really know him as Lord and Messiah until their brother Lazarus had died.

Martha said to Jesus,
  "Lord, if you had been here,
    my brother would never have died."

* * *

"Your brother will rise again," Jesus assured her.
Martha replied,
  "I know he will rise again
    in the resurrection on the last day."
Jesus told her,
  "I AM the resurrection and the life:
  whoever believes in me,
    though he should die,
    will come to life;
  and whoever is alive and believes in me
    will never die. Do you believe this?"
Martha replied,
  "Yes, Lord, I have come to believe
    that you are the Messiah, the Son of God:
    he who is to come into the world."
                                        (Jn 11:21, 23-27)

Martha felt the same awe as Peter, the Samaritan woman, the man born blind, and of course, Nathanael, when Jesus revealed himself to her as the Messiah. To each of these people Jesus let them know that he loved them and knew them. They responded in wonder and delight in being loved and known by him. They respond by loving him in return. Each one's confession of faith is foremost an act of love.

Let us return to Jesus' call of Nathanael. After Nathanael believes in Jesus as Son of God, Jesus rewards his faith by promising him,

> "You shall see the sky opened
>   and the angels of God
>   ascending and descending
>   on the Son of Man." (Jn 1:51; cf. Gn 28:12)

This is a reference to Jacob's dream at Bethel where he saw in a dream "a stairway rested on the ground with its top reaching to the heavens; and the angels were going up and down on it." And the Lord God spoke to Jacob in his dream saying,

> "I will protect you wherever you go,
>   and bring you back to this land.
> I will never leave you until I have done
>   what I have promised you."   (Gn 28:15)

When Jacob awoke from the dream, he exclaimed,

> "Indeed the Lord is in this place,
>   and I knew it not."
>   And trembling, he said,
> "How awesome is this place!
> This is none other
>   than the house of God
>   and the gate of heaven!"   (Gn 28:12, 15-16)

As Jacob was trembling in awe and wonder at finding himself in the divine presence, so did Nathanael delight in the presence of the Almighty, the Son of God — Jesus.

Jacob's dream is a dream of the presence of the Almighty. Jesus declares himself Son of God because the angels will ascend and descend upon him for he, Jesus, is *the* holy place. All divinity rests and resides in him. He is the new temple, the consecrated one, the anointed, the Messiah. Jesus says as much when he advises his adversaries,

> "Destroy this temple
> and in three days
> I will raise it up."

* * *

> Actually
> he was talking about
> the temple of his body.   (Jn 2:19-21)

The divinity of Jesus is clearly being revealed to Nathanael. Now let us turn to the symbol of the fig tree. The fig tree is the symbol of fecundity. Didn't Jesus curse the barren fig tree (cf. Mt 21:18 ff.; Mk 11:12 ff.; Lk 13:6 ff.)? When Jesus called Nathanael, he *knew* Nathanael was to be his disciple. Nathanael was called to bear very much fruit. Thus the "fig tree" is no accident or incidental. Later on Jesus would say to Nathanael and his other disciples and to us,

> "It was not you who chose me,
>   it was I who chose you
>   to go forth and bear fruit." (Jn 15:16)

And as we know, to bear fruit the grain of wheat must fall into the ground and die, lest it remain just a grain of wheat (cf. Jn 12:24). Jesus had to be the grain of wheat and die in order to rise again and send his Holy Spirit. He had to return to the Father. He says to his disciples,

> "Now that I go back
>   to him who sent me,
>   not one of you asks me,
>   'Where are you going?'
> Because I have had all this
>   to say to you,
>   you are overcome with grief.
> Yet I tell you the sober truth:
>   It is much better for you that I go.
> If I fail to go,
>   the Paraclete [Consoler]
>   will never come to you;
> Whereas if I go,
>   I will send him to you.

* * *

> When he comes, however,
>   being the Spirit of truth,
>   he will guide you to all truth.
> He will not speak on his own,
>   but he will speak only what he hears,
>   and will announce to you the things to
>   come." (Jn 16:6-7, 13)

Jesus tells us that we who bear fruit will be consoled and strengthened and enlightened by his Holy Spirit. This Holy Spirit will guide us to truth for like Jesus we are "consecrated in truth" (cf. Jn 17:17-19). In the Gospel of John there is no account of the institution of the Eucharist. Some scripture scholars have seen in this part of Jesus' priestly prayer to his Father an allusion to the institution of the Eucharist. The author of the Fourth Gospel uses the word, *hagiazo*, for the word to "consecrate." This Greek verb had the meanings "to set apart as sacred to God, to regard as sacred, to make holy, and also to purify and to cleanse." In light of these meanings Jesus reminds us that the Holy Spirit who "will guide us to all truth" will also prepare us to be "consecrated in truth." Jesus prays,

> "Consecrate them by means of truth —
>   'Your word is truth.'
> As you have sent me into the world;
>   so I have sent them into the world,
> I consecrate myself for their sakes now,
>   that they may be consecrated in truth."
>
> (Jn 17:17-19)

Jesus says that he must consecrate himself for our sakes now, that is, in his humanity he had to suffer loneliness, rejection, misunderstanding, and the treachery of betrayal before he would be raised from the dead by the power of his Father (cf. Eph

1:17-20). Jesus had to suffer death to bear fruit. So it is with each of us.

Jesus also tells us that the Holy Spirit "will announce to you the things to come." Yes, the Holy Spirit will enlighten our innermost vision revealing to us the mysteries of the kingdom, and bring to our minds the delights of the kingdom to come where

> "Eye has not seen,
>> ear has not heard,
>> nor has it so much as dawned
>> on our minds
>> what God has prepared
>> for those who love him."
> Yet God has revealed this wisdom to us
>> through the Spirit,
>> for the Spirit scrutinizes all matters,
>> even the deep things of God. (1 Cor 2:9-10)

If we bear fruit — having been "consecrated in truth" — we will inherit the kingdom whose fruits are the fruits of the Holy Spirit. These are

> love, joy, peace,
> patient endurance,
> kindness, generosity,
> faith, mildness,
> and chastity.   (Gal 5:22)

The first and supreme fruit of the Holy Spirit is love and this is the delight of the soul. St. Augustine tells us we are "drawn to God by our own will indeed, but by delight as well." If the body has delights, should there not be delights for the soul as well? If the soul has no delights how can the psalmist write,

> How precious is your kindness
>> O God!
> Your children take refuge in
>> the shadow of your wings.
> They have their fill of the prime
>> gifts of your house;
> from your delightful stream
>> you give them to drink,
> For with you is the fountain of life
>> and in your light we see light.   (Ps 36:8-10)

"The delightful stream" and "the fountain of light" are the Holy Spirit. Augustine continues,

> Give me a lover;
>> and the lover will know what I mean!
> Give me someone who desires and hungers,
>> someone who wanders in the desert
>> and thirsts for the fountain of the eternal country
>> — that person will know what I mean.
> Show a green branch to a sheep
>> and it will follow you.
> Show sweets to a child
>> and the child will follow you.
> Persons are drawn by love,
>> by ties of the heart.
> If delights draw us,
>> will not Christ draw us?

> (St. Augustine, *Commentary on John*, Treatise 26)

Delight, of course, is the Holy Spirit! Delight is to be known from all eternity by Jesus, the Son of God and the Creative Word. And we are the delight of the Godhead as the Creative Word was and is and always will be of the Father. As the sage of Proverbs describes the Creative Word as delight of the Father the sage also writes that the Word "plays" before him. That is, the Creative Word enjoys the complete freedom and joy of relationship with the Father. That is what it means to be in love. Jesus, then, is the pure joy of the Father. Before the world began Jesus, as Creative Word, knew us personally and individually in a unique relationship of love with each of us. Jesus knows us now as risen Lord in the breaking of the bread. He draws us to himself because he "like the child shown sweets" is drawn to us and delights in us as we are drawn to him and delight in him. This is what it means to be in love with God. In Jesus' delight in us he bestows the Holy Spirit upon us. And then in our wonder and joy we too can say as Nathanael,

"You are the Son of God."

As Philip sought Nathanael and aroused his curiosity to make Jesus say to him,

"Before Philip called you,
I 'knew' you under the fig tree,"

so we too must seek out Jesus and ask him for the delight of our souls, his Holy Spirit. Jesus says to us,

"Ask and you shall receive;
  seek and you shall find;
  knock and it shall be opened unto you.
For whoever asks, receives;
  whoever seeks, finds;
  whoever knocks is admitted.
What father among you
  will give his child a snake
    if the child asks for a fish,
  or hand the child a scorpion
    if he asks for an egg?
If you with all your sins
  know how to give your children good
things,
  how much more will the heavenly Father
  give the Holy Spirit to those who ask him."
(Lk 11:9-13)

The risen Jesus extends the image of the one who knocks and applies it to himself. He says,

"Behold!
I stand at the door and knock.
If anyone hears me calling
  and opens the door,
I will enter his house
  and sup with him
  and he with me."   (Rv 3:20)

When Jesus offers himself and his holy and risen Spirit to us in the sacrament of his body and blood, he delights in us and we in him. In each Eucharist he knows us as he knew Nathanael. In each Eucharist we bear fruit as if he "saw" us or "knew" us "under the fig tree." In each Eucharist we are drawn to the risen Jesus and he to us. In each Eucharist the risen Jesus with his Father and Holy Spirit are to us the supreme delight, the "*mentis*[1] *jubilatio!*" (St. Thomas Aquinas, *Lauda, Sion, Salvatorem*). "*Mentis jubilatio,*" the Eucharist, is the delight of the heart and the jubilee of the soul!

---

[1] It is well to explain here Thomas Aquinas' use of the nouns *ratio* and *mens* meaning mind. *Ratio* is simply the activity of reason. *Mens*, however, is more complex and inclusive. *Mens* contains the concepts of *spiritus* (spirit) and *anima* (soul). *Mens* is the activity of the mind or spirit or soul or heart which grasps or knows the experience of poetry or prayer.

THE HOLY SPIRIT AS FIREBRAND

The "Wild Flush"

The Lord said to Samuel:
"How long will you grieve for Saul,
    whom I have rejected as king of Israel?
Fill your horn with oil, and be on your way.
I am sending you to Jesse of Bethlehem,
    for I have chosen my king from among his
sons."

       * * *

Jesse presented seven sons before Samuel,
    but Samuel said to Jesse,
"The Lord had not chosen any one of these."
Then Samuel asked Jesse,
"Are these all the sons you have?"
Jesse replied,
"There is still the youngest who is tending
sheep."

       * * *

Jesse sent and had the young man brought to
them.
He was ruddy, a youth handsome to behold
    and making a splendid appearance.
The Lord said,
"There anoint him, for this is he!"
Then Samuel, with the horn of oil in his hand,
    anointed him in the midst of his brothers;
and from that day on,
    the spirit of the Lord rushed upon David.
               (1 S 16:1, 10-13)

We read that in the call and election of David the spirit of the Lord "rushed" upon David. Did this overflowing and overwhelming torrent terrify David or send him into ecstasy? The author of First Samuel is silent about David's reaction and we are only left to wonder how David felt as the spirit of the Lord rushed upon him.

After the centuries had passed and after the agony of the exile we read again of the Holy Spirit as announced not by a seer or prophet but by the angel Gabriel to "a virgin betrothed to a man named Joseph, of the house of David. The virgin's name was Mary" (Lk 1:27). Although we are all too familiar with the account of the annunciation of the birth of the Messiah, it is well to re-examine the text in the Gospel of Luke.

> Upon arriving the angel said to Mary:
> "Rejoice, O highly favored daughter!
> The Lord is with you.
> Blessed are you among women."
> She was deeply troubled by his words,
>   and wondered what the greeting meant.
> The angel went on to say to her:
> "Do not fear, Mary.
> You have found favor with God.
> You shall conceive and bear a son
>   and give him the name Jesus."
> Mary said to the angel,
> "How can this be
>   since I do not know man?"
> The angel answered her:

The Holy Spirit as Firebrand

"The Holy Spirit will come upon you
    and the power of the Most High
    will overshadow you;
hence the holy offspring to be born
    will be called Son of God."

(Lk 1:28-31, 34-35)

Mary is "deeply troubled." The Holy Spirit descends upon her or rushed upon her causing her fear and fright. The Holy Spirit is disturbing — creating unrest in the Blessed Virgin Mary. This is not the image we usually contemplate when we think of the angel Gabriel greeting Mary. The famous Fra Angelico "Annunciations" always picture Mary as receptive and in repose. Byzantine iconography, however, usually pictures Mary with her hand held up resisting the angel or Holy Spirit. William Butler Yeats captures this feeling of fright and terror in Mary. The poet writes,

The threefold terror of love; a
        fallen flare
Through the hollow of an ear;
Wings beating about the room;
The terror of all terrors that I bore
The Heavens in my womb.

(William Butler Yeats, "The Mother of God")

The "threefold terror of love" is the Godhead — Father, Son, and Spirit, and the Spirit is called a "fallen flare" — a firebrand coming into the Virgin Mary's ear "open to obedience" (Ps 40:7). The

Angel's "wings beating around the room" suggest the vehement action of the Holy Spirit. Wouldn't any young maiden be overwhelmed to bear the Christ or, as Yeats says, "the Heavens" in her womb?

The Holy Spirit is a firebrand to Mary causing, at one and the same time, unrest, violence, excitement, ecstasy, and joy — joy which could not be contained. After the angel left her, Mary — moved by the Holy Spirit — "set out in haste into the hill country to a town of Judah" to tell her cousin Elizabeth the terror and the ecstasy she experienced.

> When Elizabeth heard Mary's greeting,
>   the baby leapt in her womb.
> Elizabeth was filled with the Holy Spirit
>   and cried out in a loud voice:
> "Blest are you among women
>   and blest is the fruit of your womb.
> But who am I
>   that the mother of my Lord
>   should come to me?
> The moment your greeting
>   sounded in my ears,
>   the baby leapt in my womb for joy.
> Blest is she who trusted
>   that the Lord's words to her
>   would be fulfilled." (Lk 1:41-45)

Not only is Mary moved by the Holy Spirit, but Elizabeth her kinswoman is also "filled with the Holy Spirit." Mary's terror turned to joy overflowing. Again the Holy Spirit prompted her response. Because Mary responded to the angel,

"I am the servant of the Lord.
Let it be done to me as you say,"   (Lk 1:38)

the terror of "wings beating about the room" gave way to serenity and ecstasy. As the spirit of God breathed over the waters changing the dark abyss of the formless void into the order of the heavens and the earth and all their array (cf. Gn 1:1, 2:1), so the confusion and almost chaotic turmoil in Mary caused by the Spirit gave way to tranquility also caused by the same Spirit. Mary could then utter her canticle of praise.

"My being proclaims
    the greatness of the Lord,
my spirit finds joy
    in God my savior;
For he has looked upon his servant
    in her lowliness;
all ages to come
    shall call me blessed.
God who is mighty
    has done great things for me,
holy is his name."   (Lk 1:46-49)

The spirit of the Lord rushed upon Mary like an overflowing torrent. The suggestion of vehemence forged virginity into maternity — and terror into serenity. And in like manner the energy of the Holy Spirit forges us the barren into the fruitful. We are transformed by Love, for Love, in Love.

Later the Spirit of the Lord would rush upon

Jesus at his baptism in the Jordan making him aware that he was the suffering servant of Yahweh, and again at his transfiguration giving him ineffable consolation and a foretaste of his glory before he "set his face for Jerusalem" (Lk 9:51). The Spirit would also rush upon Jesus at the moment of his death, resurrection, glorification, and sending of the Spirit.

Gerard Manley Hopkins describes this mystery using the image of the rose and blossom.

> Is Mary the rose, then? Mary the tree?
> But the blossom, the blossom there,
>   who can it be?
> Who can her rose be? It could be but one:
> Christ Jesus, our Lord, her God and
>   her son.
> What was the colour of that blossom bright?
> White to begin with, immaculate white.
> But what a wild flush on the flake of
>   it stood
> When the rose ran in crimsonings
>   down the cross-wood!
>
> (Gerard Manley Hopkins, "*Rosa Mystica*")

Is Mary the rose? Is Jesus the rose? They are one this is the mystery of the virginal divine maternity. Yet Jesus is the blossom — immaculate white — until the "wild flush" of the Holy Spirit sends Jesus, the immaculate white blossom into the crucible of love and changes and transforms him into the red rose at the moment of his martyrdom. At the moment of martyrdom the Holy Spirit all at once accepts Jesus' sacrifice and allows Jesus "to hand over his spirit" (cf. Jn 19:30) to his disciples and unleash the power and peace of the Spirit upon a waiting world. The "wild flush" of the Spirit allows Jesus to give that same Spirit to us as an overflowing torrent and river of peace issuing from the open side of Jesus. "When the rose ran in crimsonings down the cross-wood," the work of redemption was accomplished and the Holy Spirit was bestowed upon us by the all-at-once crucified, risen and glorified Christ. This "wild flush" or rush of the Holy Spirit upon Jesus is simultaneously the violent mystery of the terror and agony of Jesus in his death, and the serenity and tranquility of the Father's accepting his sacrifice and glorifying him as Lord and sender of the Spirit. Like Mary Jesus knew terror and tranquility. In his agony where "his sweat became like drops of blood" (Lk 22:44), and on the cross where he cried out in anguish,

> "My God, my God, why
> have you forsaken me?"   (Mt 27:46)

the Spirit rushed upon Jesus causing him terror. And the Spirit also showed the "immeasurable scope of his power... in raising Christ from the dead and seating him at the right hand of the Father" (Eph 1:19-20). The "wild flush" or the rush of the Holy Spirit is all at once terror and delight in Jesus. The Holy Spirit is the firebrand causing anguish and unrest and the peace and joy of the resurrection. The first recorded words of Jesus to his disciples after his resurrection are

> "Peace be with you."

> When he had said this,
>   he showed them his hands and his side.
> At the sight of the Lord the disciples rejoiced.
>   "Peace be with you," he said again.

* * *

> Then he breathed on them and said:
>   "Receive the Holy Spirit."   (Jn 20:19-22)

Jesus gives the Holy Spirit to us as his Easter gift with the promise of peace. But we know "the wild flush" will also come to us with terror — with his awesome might. Jesus tells his disciples,

> "See, I send down upon you
>   the promise of my Father.
> Remain here in the city [Jerusalem]
>   until you are clothed with power
>   from on high."   (Lk 24:49)

"The power from on high" is both dread and delight as we have discovered in the experience of Mary and Jesus. Should it not be the same with us?

As the disciples and Mary, the mother of Jesus, entered the city and went to an upstairs room, they waited for the "fulfillment of the Father's promise" (cf. Ac 1:14 and Ac 1:4). The "fulfillment of the Father's promise" is, of course, the Holy Spirit. As Mary was waiting for the Pentecost event, did she not remember her first experience of that "fallen flare" when the Holy Spirit overwhelmed her with terror? Would this encounter with that "wild flush" be different? Would the Spirit rush upon her with dread or delight or both? Yes, as "daughter of her only Son" (*Paradiso*, xxxiii) she would remember the ominous prophesy of Simeon,

> "Your own soul
>   a sword shall pierce."   (Lk 2:35)

And as spouse of the Holy Spirit she could say in ecstasy,

> I am espoused to him whom
>   angels serve,
> Upon whose beauty sun and
>   moon in wonder gaze.   (Office of St. Agnes)

Mary sat waiting for the Holy Spirit remembering the greeting of the archangel Gabriel, her confusion and Joseph's confusion, her visit to her cousin Elizabeth, the joy and pain of her son's birth, the wonder of the shepherds and the adoration of the Magi. She remembered Simeon's words and Anna's joy as she gave thanks at beholding her son the Messiah. She recalled her going to Jerusalem each year at Passover and that one year when she lost her son and sought him in sorrow. Didn't she lose her son again in Jerusalem at Passover as they mocked him, and scourged him, spit upon him, and crucified him? She also remembered the wedding feast at Cana and the wonder she felt as she watched her son change water into wine. And she remembered when his hour had come and how she stood in grief at the foot of the cross. She remembered how she caressed his head and his hair matted with blood as she held him after he had been taken down from the cross. She remembered the unspeakable grief of placing his body in a tomb sealed by a stone. And she remembered the wide-eyed surprise of beholding his risen and glorified body. "Mary treasured all these things and reflected on them in her heart" (Lk 2:19).

The Holy Spirit rushes upon us, too, energizing us and sometimes devastating us. The Holy Spirit is a firebrand in our lives causing us unrest and unspeakable joy. His power is abundant and lavish and prodigal. The Holy Spirit ignites us with love and when we drink deeply of the Spirit we know the thrill of joyful inebriation. The Holy Spirit inflames and excites us with terror and tranquility as he did in the lives of Jesus and Mary. He consumes us and, like the blossom immaculate white, we too experience the "wild flush" that sets us aflame branding our psyche and searing and sealing our souls with a sacred stigmata. This fire is a torment to the self-serving, a purgation to the penitent, and an ecstasy to the blessed.

> The dove descending breaks the air
> With flame of incandescent terror
> of which tongues declare
> The one discharge from sin and error.
> The only hope, or else despair
> Lies in the choice of pyre or pyre —
> To be redeemed from fire by fire.
>
> Who then devised the torment? Love.
> Love is the unfamiliar Name
> Behind the hands that wove
> The intolerable shirt of flame
> Which human power cannot remove
> We only live, only suspire
> Consumed by either fire or fire.
>
> (T.S. Eliot, "Little Gidding" IV,
> from *The Four Quartets*)

Eliot tells us that Love devised the torment. And Gerard Manley Hopkins tells us "the rose [is] in a mystery." To be redeemed from the fire of purgation into the fire of ecstasy is the mystery of Love. And Love is the mystery of the Holy Spirit. This is the mystery of ecstasy — complete intimacy with the Holy Spirit. This ecstasy is only experienced after being ravished by that Spirit — completely suffused by him as firebrand. Only when the Holy Spirit ravishes us as a "wild flush" will "the fire and the rose be one."

With the drawing of this Love and
    the voice of this Calling
We shall not cease from our
    exploration
And at the end of all our exploring
Will be to arrive where we started
And know the place for the very
    first time.

* * *

And all shall be well and
All manner of thing shall be well
When tongues of flame are
    in-folded
Into the crowned knot of fire
And the fire and the rose are one.

(T.S. Eliot, "Little Gidding" V, from *The Four Quartets*)

Hopkins again expresses this mystery of Love. Of the "blossom," Christ, and of us who are also part of the mystery of the rose, he writes,

How many leaves had it? Five they
    were then,
Five like the senses and members of men,
Five is their number by nature, but
    now,
They multiply, multiply, who can tell
    how?
Does it smell sweet too in that holy
    place? —
Sweet unto God, and the sweetness
    is grace:
O breath of it bathes great heaven
    above,

The Holy Spirit as Firebrand

> In grace that is charity, grace that is
> love.
>
> (Gerard Manley Hopkins, "*Rosa Mystica*")

Hopkins begins the poem intriguing us stating,

> "the rose in a mystery"
>
> ("*Rosa Mystica*")

And yes, in that mystery we too are drawn into the "wild flush" of the Holy Spirit. We are the five "leaves" or five wounds of Christ that "multiply." "Who can tell how?" We know how Christ's wounds multiply "in grace that is charity, grace that is love." Our wounds commingle with his until our blood too "runs in crimsonings down the cross-wood."

As the "wild flush" of the Holy Spirit surges into us driving us into dread or delight, terror or tranquility, we are ravished into ecstasy where as the rose we remain fresh, fragrant, fecund, and moist yet consumed by flames of fire as the mystery of the burning bush or the "crowned knot of fire." At each Eucharist the "wild flush" rushes upon us and surges within us. This is the "threefold terror of love" and love is a mystery, like the rose. And as the rose and the fire are one, we are one with the Holy Spirit. And this union is called mystical marriage. In each Eucharist the Holy Spirit surges within us and the surge is often gentle. The Holy Spirit may come mightily as a driving wind and peals of thunder amid trumpet blasts (cf. Ac 2:2; Ex 19:16-19), but much more often the Holy Spirit comes sweetly in the bread that is the breath that Jesus breathed into us as he said,

"Receive the Holy Spirit."　　　　(Jn 20:22)

The peace of the Holy Spirit is Jesus' Easter gift to us. The Holy Spirit is the "fulfillment of the Father's promise" (Ac 1:4). In the bread that is life and breath that is sweet refreshment — we are always becoming the spouse of the Holy Spirit. We are no longer forsaken and desolate, but we are called the Holy Spirit's delight and thus we are espoused to him (cf. Is 62:4).

In the bread that is breath and life, in the bread that is the Spirit of the risen Jesus we are "sealed with the Holy Spirit… the pledge of our inheritance and the first payment against our full redemption to praise God's glory" (Eph 1:13 b-14). As the Spirit gently surges in us we are being raised to new life and the Spirit shows us "the immeasurable scope of his power in us who believe. It is like the power he showed in raising Christ from the dead" (Eph 1:19-20). The surging of the Spirit is the sweetness of an espousal. In the bread that is breath and life the Spirit's surging is the invitation to be his bride, his chosen, his beloved, his delight. The Spirit bids us,

The Holy Spirit as Firebrand

Surge, propera, et veni!
Arise, hasten, and come!

> (from "*Tota Pulchra Es*,"[1] ancient Marian chant)

---

[1] "You are all beautiful, O Mary!"